D0516899

GREAT EVENTS

Photo credits:

Jonathan Wallen: Page 9
AP/Wide World Photo: Cover; Pages 26, 29
Archive Photos: Pages 10-11, 11, 13, 14, 18, 19, 22, 24
Archive/Michael Berson: Page 25
Archive Photos/Express Newspapers: Page 27
Archive Photos/Frank Driggs Collection: Page 21-22
Archive Photos/Museum of the City of New York: Pages 21-22
Archive Photos/New York Times Co./Robert Walker: Page 27
Archive Photos/Reuters/Dennis Paquin: Page 29
Hulton-Deutsch Collection/Corbis-Bettmann: Page 21
Wally McNamee/Corbis-Bettmann: Page 27
UPI/Corbis-Bettmann: Pages 26, 28
Corbis-Bettmann: Cover; Pages 7, 8, 11, 12, 12-13, 15, 16, 17, 22, 23, 25, 26, 27
Christopher R. Harris/Globe Photo: Page 28
Granger Collection: Cover; Pages 6, 6-7, 7, 8-9, 9, 10, 11, 12, 13,14, 15, 16, 16-17, 18, 19, 20, 22, 23, 24, Endpages
Hulton-Getty Images: Pages 14, 16, 19
NASA: Page 25

Copyright © 1999
Kidsbooks, Inc.
3535 West Peterson Ave.
Chicago, IL 60659

Manufactured in the United States of America

Visit us at www.kidsbooks.com
Volume discounts available for group purchases.

EYES ON AMERICA™

GREAT EVENTS

Written by
Tracy Christopher, Ph.D.

kidsbooks Incorporated

LAND HO!

In 1492, Christopher Columbus sailed the ocean blue, and reached the Bahamas—which he thought were islands mentioned in Marco Polo's travelogues of Asia. Columbus had found a "New World"—a continent unknown to Europeans. His discovery prompted generations of explorers to sail for what would later be called the Americas.

King Ferdinand and Queen Isabella of Spain financed Columbus's expedition of 1492.

FINDING FLORIDA

Until Juan Ponce de Léon set out from Puerto Rico in 1513, looking for the fountain of eternal youth, no explorer had seen the land that would later be known as the continental United States. On Easter Sunday, Ponce de Léon discovered what he thought was another island. He named it La Florida, after the Spanish term for Easter Sunday—*Pascua florida*, or "flowery feast."

TOUGH BEGINNINGS

In 1607, three small ships sent by an English corporation landed at Chesapeake Bay. They wintered at a site they named Jamestown, after King James I. By 1610, disease, Indian raids, and starvation had devastated the population. Only 2,000 of the first 10,000 Virginia settlers survived.

THE PILGRIMS ARRIVE

Of the 103 passengers aboard the *Mayflower* (*below*) in 1620, only 35 were Pilgrims seeking freedom from England's Anglican Church. The others were looking for adventure and business opportunities.

◄ AMERICA'S FIRST WRITTEN LAWS

Before landing at Plymouth Rock, Massachusetts, the *Mayflower* colonists wrote and signed the Mayflower Compact. It said that no decision could be made without the consent of the majority—a key principle of American democracy.

▲ THANKSGIVING #1

The *Mayflower* colonists landed at the worst time of year for building, planting, and hunting. The area's Wampanoag Indians helped them survive. The following year, 50 colonists and 90 Wampanoags celebrated a successful harvest by feasting on deer, turkey, corn, squash, pumpkins (most of which were new foods for Europeans).

WHAT A STEAL!

In 1626, the Dutch West India Company bought Man-hattan Island and Long Island for some beads and goods said to be worth $24! Most Native Americans believed that land belonged to the gods: It could be used and shared, but not owned. When Indians signed treaties selling their land, they didn't expect to lose their homelands forever.

THE REVOLUTION

The American Revolution (1775-1783), involving about 300,000 colonial soldiers, swelled into a conflict that stretched to the American frontier and beyond. With the victory over Britain, a new nation was born.

Crispus Attucks, a former slave, took part in rebelling against the British. He was the first man killed in the Boston Massacre.

A TAXING PROBLEM

By 1750, there were 13 colonies with 2.5 million people in America. In 1765, when Britain began to levy taxes on tea and on legal documents—called stamps—colonists called for "no taxation without representation." (The colonists could not vote for members of Parliament, Britain's government.)

BOSTON MASSACRE

To combat rebelliousness over taxes, Britain sent two regiments to Boston in 1768, and ordered Bostonians to house and feed the troops. On March 5, 1770, as a crowd of unarmed colonists jeered at the hated "redcoats," the soldiers opened fire. Five people were killed. News of this "Boston Massacre" spread, feeding resentment against British rule.

BIG TEA PARTY

As a protest, citizens of Boston refused to buy the highly taxed British tea. Eventually, they refused to unload it from ships. The royal governor set a deadline of midnight on December 16, 1773: Unload the tea, or else! That night, 50 patriots disguised as Indians dumped 342 chests of tea, weighing 320 pounds each, into the harbor.

8

A DECLARATION

On July 4, 1776, colonial representatives signed the Declaration of Independence. Written in just three weeks by Thomas Jefferson, the Declaration of Independence described a desire for self-rule, as well as the ideal that government should defend its citizens' rights to life, liberty, and the pursuit of happiness.

FIRST SHOTS

On April 19, 1775, the first shot of the American Revolution was fired at Lexington, Massachusetts. By day's end, 250 British redcoats and 90 American patriots were dead. Poet Ralph Waldo Emerson later called it "the shot heard round the world"— a symbol of struggles for independence everywhere.

CROSSING THE DELAWARE

In October 1776, the army of General George Washington clashed with superior British forces at White Plains, New York. Forced to retreat, the Americans crossed the Delaware River into Pennsylvania. On December 25, 1776, Washington recrossed the river with 2,400 men and marched to Trenton, New Jersey, where he surprised British troops. This Christmas Day victory greatly boosted American morale.

A NEW GOVERNMENT

After researching hundreds of books, James Madison drafted the Constitution and presented it at the Constitutional Convention in Philadelphia, Pennsylvania, in May 1787. This blueprint for a new government called for all citizens to be treated equally—a first in world history.

FIRST PRESIDENT

Toward the end of the Revolution, many of Washington's officers urged him to seize power and rule as king. Washington refused. Elected the first U.S. president, he was inaugurated in New York City on April 30, 1789.

FOR OUR RIGHTS

Delegates to the 1787 convention provided ways to amend the Constitution. The first 10 amendments, known as the Bill of Rights, were adopted in 1791 to guarantee individual liberties, including freedom of speech and of religion.

A NEW NATION'S NEW CAPITAL

The first U.S. capital was New York, then Philadelphia. In 1790, a site was chosen and a new capital city built—named in honor of the first president. Both House and Senate occupied the Capitol building, which was just down the road from a mansion for the president.

◀ THE WAR OF 1812

Britain was slow to acknowledge the loss of its colonies. During its war with France, Britain attacked U.S. ships and captured their sailors—so U.S. President James Madison declared war in 1812. The U.S. victory put a stop to Britain's aspirations in America.

On June 14, 1777, the Second Continental Congress adopted a flag with 13 stripes and 13 stars to represent the 13 original colonies.

LIBERTY BELL

On July 8, 1776, Philadelphia's 2,000-pound Liberty Bell rang in loud peals from what later was called Independence Hall, where the Declaration of Independence had just been ratified (approved).

THE WHITE HOUSE

During the war of 1812, British troops invaded Washington, setting fire to the Capitol, the President's House, and other key buildings. After the President's House was fixed and repainted white to cover the scorch marks, it was dubbed the White House.

11

SPANNING THE CONTINENT

In 1803, the size of the United States doubled when President Thomas Jefferson paid $15 million to gain 828,000 square miles of land from France. The Louisiana Purchase, as it is known, stretched from the Mississippi River to the Rocky Mountains. It was the greatest single addition of land to the United States.

Lewis and Clark with their guide, Sacagawea.

LEWIS & CLARK

Meriwether Lewis and William Clark headed up the Mississippi River on May 14, 1804, with 30 men in a flatboat and two canoes to explore the huge Louisiana Territory. That expedition, which lasted two years and covered 8,000 miles, provided valuable maps and journals that opened the American West to white settlers.

WILDERNESS ROAD ▲

Eastern forests were once so dense that a squirrel might go from the Atlantic Ocean to the Ohio River without touching the ground. But on the far side of the Appalachian Mountains were the fields of Kentucky—easier land to farm. Daniel Boone blazed a trail through the mountains, and led groups of settlers westward. By 1790, almost 200,000 people had traveled the 300 miles of Boone's Wilderness Road into Kentucky—and beyond.

TRANSCONTINENTAL RR

The Pacific Railroad Act, signed by President Abraham Lincoln in 1862, gave federal money and land for extending the railroad from Nebraska to California. Working from both ends, laborers laid track until the two teams met on May 10, 1869, at Promontory Point, Utah (*in background photo*). Passengers could then travel at 25 mph from the East Coast to Sacramento—once a six-month ordeal—in a mere 10 days.

FULTON'S STEAMBOAT ▶

Robert Fulton was the first American to create a reliable paddle-wheeled steamboat—the *Clermont*. On August 18, 1807, it steamed 150 miles up the Hudson River from New York City to Albany in under 33 hours. Hundreds of Fulton's steamboats were soon moving up the Mississippi River, the widest and longest waterway in North America.

THE ERIE CANAL ▼

When completed in 1824, the Erie Canal linked the Atlantic Ocean with Lake Erie, and took passengers and freight as far west as Ohio three or four times as fast as overland routes. Four feet deep and 40 feet wide, the canal traversed 360 miles.

◀ "REMEMBER THE ALAMO!"

In 1836, Mexican leader Antonio López de Santa Anna marched a 3,000-man army into Texas, long a province of Mexico. He hoped to run off American settlers. But 200 Americans, including frontiersmen Davy Crockett and Jim Bowie, stayed and fought back at an old mission called the Alamo. Only six survived. Enraged Americans went to war with Mexico in 1846, with the battle cry "Remember the Alamo!" Mexico lost, and was forced to give up land all the way to the West Coast.

UNITING THE STATES

As new states were admitted to the Union, the issue of slavery threatened to divide the country. The mostly agricultural South argued that each state had the right to decide whether it would allow slavery. The industrial North pushed for the federal government to ban slavery. In 1861, the issue of states' rights versus individual liberty erupted into civil war.

At the start of the Civil War, four million slaves lived in America, three million of them in the South.

UNCLE TOM'S CABIN

In 1852, Harriet Beecher Stowe wrote *Uncle Tom's Cabin*, a novel that stirred up powerful antislavery feelings at home and abroad. In 1863, upon meeting Stowe, author of the most influential American book of the 19th century, President Lincoln remarked: "So this is the little lady who wrote the book that made this great war."

135,000 SETS, 270,000 VOLUMES SOLD.

UNCLE TOM'S CABIN

R SALE HERE.

The Greatest Book of the Age.

UNDERGROUND RAILROAD

Congress made many compromises to keep peace. The Fugitive Slave Laws of 1793 and 1850 required people to capture and return escaped slaves. The Underground Railroad was an organization of people called "conductors" who helped slaves reach Canada, where they could be free.

Harriet Tubman helped so many ▶ slaves escape that she was known as "the Moses of her people." She also served as a nurse, cook, scout, and Union spy during the Civil War.

THE SECESSION

Abraham Lincoln had spoken out against slavery. Soon after he was elected president in 1860, 11 slave states seceded (withdrew) from the United States. When Confederate troops fired on Fort Sumter on April 12, 1861, Lincoln realized that nothing short of civil war could reunite the Union.

EMANCIPATION

On September 22, 1862, President Lincoln issued his Emancipation Proclamation, which declared all slaves in Confederate states free as of January 1, 1863. This important act struck a blow to the South. With a moral cause as one of the Union's official goals, Lincoln's proclamation made foreign powers reluctant to aid the Confederacy.

A tireless leader, Lincoln made many visits to field headquarters. The Civil War ended on April 9, 1865, but Lincoln had little time to enjoy peace. On April 14, 1865, John Wilkes Booth shot the President at Ford's Theater in Washington. Lincoln died the next day.

STAGGERING LOSSES ▼

Men rushed to enlist in "the 90-day" war, sure that it would be over in no time. More than 500,000 Americans died in the Civil War (1861-1865) and more than 300,000 were wounded. More than 50,000 Union and Confederate troops were killed or wounded in a single battle: the three-day ordeal at Gettysburg.

◄ BLACK CODES

For a brief time during Reconstruction (1865-1877), blacks were allowed the right to vote. But eventually Southern state governments voted in laws called Black Codes, which deprived African-Americans of basic rights, including the rights to vote and to serve on juries. It took a century of struggle to reverse those injustices.

LAND OF OPPORTUNITY

In 1862, Congress passed the Homestead Act. For a mere $10, all citizens—including women and immigrants—could have 160 acres of public land each, if they farmed the land for at least five years. The government sometimes held a "land rush" (*in background photo*). At a gunshot or other signal, people were allowed to ride into new territory to claim land—and finders were keepers. Between 1860 and 1890, more U.S. land was turned into farmland than in all the years from 1607 to 1860.

These settlers, who acquired their land as a result of the Homestead Act, pose outside their farmhouse on the prairie.

In 1838, U.S. troops forced 20,000 Cherokees to walk through winter storms from their home territory in the southeast to what is now part of Oklahoma. One in four Cherokees died during the trek, known as the Trail of Tears.

NATIVE NATIONS

In 1776, when the colonists declared themselves a nation, there were 250 Native American nations, with a total population in the millions, living on lands from the East Coast to the Pacific Ocean. As European immigrants and other pioneers made claims to more and more of that land, armed conflict became inevitable. By 1890, the total Indian population had fallen to 228,000.

GOING WEST

In 1843, 120 Conestoga prairie schooners left Independence, Missouri, and headed for the Oregon Territory. Moving at a pace of only 1 to 15 miles per day, it took that first wagon train almost six months to travel 2,000 miles.

THE GOLD RUSH

On January 24, 1848, James Marshall spied yellow flakes in John Sutter's creek: gold! Word of the discovery traveled quickly to the East Coast and to Asia. About 85,000 prospectors flocked to California, whose population exploded from 14,000 people in 1848 to 225,000 in 1852.

WOUNDED KNEE

In 1876, General George Custer and his cavalry were massacred by Sioux warriors at the Battle of Little Bighorn (*left*). In 1890, U.S. troops—probably in revenge—killed more than 300 Sioux at Wounded Knee Creek, South Dakota. That was the last major clash between the U.S. Army and American Indians.

YELLOWSTONE

Yellowstone National Park, the country's first national park, was established in 1872, as Congress realized that the frontier was disappearing into farmland and settled communities. There are now 360 national parks and wildlife refuges.

AMERICAN KNOW-HOW

American ingenuity sparked a machine age that transformed the nation's farm economy, and multiplied its wealth five times between 1860 and 1890. The explosion of new inventions changed the face of America—and the world.

COTTON GIN ▲

In 1793, schoolteacher Eli Whitney introduced a "cotton engine" that could remove seeds 50 times faster than doing so by hand. However, Whitney's cotton gin had the unexpected result of encouraging slavery and keeping the South rural, as plantation owners sought more and cheaper labor to farm their ever-larger fields in the land of cotton.

▲ GEM OF A REAPER

With a hand-held scythe, a farmer working all day could harvest a single acre of wheat. Cyrus McCormick's horse-drawn reaper could harvest that acre in minutes. At an industrial fair held in London in 1851, the McCormick reaper drew more admirers than the famous Koh-i-noor diamond.

INSTANT NEWS

It took painter and inventor Samuel F. B. Morse 12 years to develop a way to send messages in code using electrical impulses. In 1844, the first message in Morse code was sent from the Supreme Court in Washington, D.C., to Baltimore, Maryland. By 1861, Morse's telegraph spanned the continent—and news could be sent from coast to coast in minutes.

ELECTRIC WONDERS

At Chicago's 1893 Columbian Exposition, some 27 million visitors admired American technological wonders powered by electricity. George Ferris's revolving wheel, which held more than 1,000 riders, was the biggest attraction. That exposition inspired the creation of theme parks in America.

▼ FLYING HIGH

On December 17, 1903, Wilbur and Orville Wright kept a small, engine-powered biplane aloft over the beach at Kitty Hawk, North Carolina, for 59 seconds. In 1927, Charles Lindbergh took aviation a big step further by being the first to fly solo across the Atlantic Ocean.

◄ NEW WHEELS

Henry Ford designed his first car in 1896. In 1908, he created a standard, easy-to-assemble design for his Model T, which he mass-produced and sold at prices that most Americans could afford. In 1924, the ten millionth Model T rolled off Ford's assembly line.

WIZARD OF INVENTION ►

Thomas Alva Edison's inventions—the electric light bulb, motion-picture camera, storage battery, and phonograph, among others—led to a better quality of life for most Americans. Edison held 1,093 patents when he died.

TO THE CITY

Between 1830 and 1930, more than 37 million immigrants entered the U.S.—the largest movement of people to one geographical region in the history of the world. To make room, the cities grew rapidly—up as well as out. In 1880, 28 percent of Americans lived in cities. Less than 100 years later, 75 percent were city dwellers.

An Italian immigrant family arriving in the U.S. in 1905.

THE STATUE OF LIBERTY

Erected on a small island and dedicated in 1886, the Statue of Liberty was the first monument most immigrants saw as they entered New York Harbor. The statue—a gift from France to the U.S.—symbolizes the spirit of individual rights and freedom.

On September 5, 1882, more than 30,000 workers marched down New York's Fifth Avenue to Union Square. Labor Day became a national holiday in 1894.

WORKERS' RIGHTS

In the late 1880s, Samuel Gompers and other labor leaders organized workers into trade unions. Eventually, the unions forced industries to grant an eight-hour workday, a five-day work week, better working conditions, and the right to negotiate wages and benefits.

20

RISING SKYLINES

With the flood of new arrivals, cities needed more home and work space. Older cities, such as New York and Chicago, had little room to grow out, so they went up. Two new developments made that possible: steel beams, which could support immense weight with a relatively small base, and the invention of safe elevators, which made the sky the limit for building height. Ever-taller skyscrapers dwarfed their neighbors, dramatically changing city skylines.

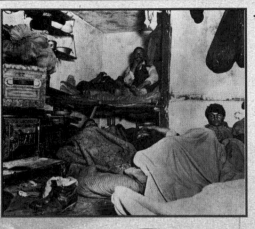

◀ URBAN REFORMS

Overcrowding and crushing poverty were problems in some cities. In 1890, journalist Jacob Riis published a book called *How the Other Half Lives*. Its heart-rending photographs of New York slum life prompted Theodore Roosevelt, a city official and future president, to burst into Riis's office to ask, "What do we do first?" The book sparked the first organized efforts to improve life in city slums.

THE JUNGLE

In 1906, Upton Sinclair published a best-selling novel, *The Jungle*. The book's criticism of the meat-packing industry's inhumane and unsanitary methods shocked the nation. Public outrage led to the passage of food-inspection laws and many other reforms.

HARLEM RENAISSANCE

Few factories in the North would hire blacks until World War I created a need for labor. Then, in what is known as the Black Migration, many African-Americans left the South for higher-paying jobs in northern cities. This population boom led to the Harlem Renaissance, a flowering of creative expression among black writers, musicians, and other artists.

During the Harlem Renaissance, white audiences flocked to clubs in Harlem, a black neighborhood in New York, to be entertained by jazz musicians, such as Duke Ellington (*at center, with baton*) and his band.

NATIONAL REFORM

Mark Twain and fellow writer Charles Dudley Warren named their era the "Gilded Age," characterizing the late 1800s as a time of ridiculous excess. While wealthy industrialists such as William Vanderbilt could afford to throw a party costing $200,000, the average factory worker in 1876 earned $500 for a full year's work.

The Vanderbilt mansion on Fifth Avenue in New York City.

EXPOSING THE RICH

Journalist Ida Tarbell spent four years writing books that exposed the unscrupulous business practices John D. Rockefeller (*left*) had used to gain control of 90 percent of the nation's oil industry. In 1906, citing Tarbell's research, the Supreme Court dissolved Rockefeller's Standard Oil trust.

WOMEN WANT THE VOTE!

In July 1848, Elizabeth Cady Stanton and Lucretia Mott held the first women's-rights convention in America. Participants drew up a declaration that called for equal rights for women in marriage, education, employment, and politics. Attracting little more than ridicule at the time, the convention launched a protest movement that, in 1920, finally won women the right to vote.

"BLACK THURSDAY"

On Thursday, October 24, 1929, the U.S. stock market crashed with dizzying speed. By 1932, at least 12 million people, one third of the nation's workforce, had lost their jobs and life savings. There were no welfare programs or unemployment insurance at that time, so the unemployed were soon homeless and hungry. This Great Depression lasted 10 long and bitter years.

$100 WILL BUY THIS CAR MUST HAVE CASH LOST ALL ON THE STOCK MARKET

A monthly check to you—

FOR THE REST OF YOUR LIFE · · BEGINNING WHEN YOU ARE 65

GET YOUR SOCIAL SECURITY ACCOUNT NUMBER promptly

APPLICATIONS ARE BEING DISTRIBUTED AT ALL WORK PLACES

Your monthly Social Security check

WHO IS ELIGIBLE · · · EVERYBODY WORKING FOR SALARY OR WAGES
(WITH ONLY A FEW EXCEPTIONS, SUCH AS AGRICULTURE, DOMESTIC SERVICE, AND

DUST BOWL ▲

Between 1909 and 1932, steel plows broke up 32 million acres of plains that bison once roamed, breaking up the sod so well that the topsoil crumbled to a fine dust. Between 1931 and 1937, America's heartland experienced the worst drought on record. Ten states were affected; the worst hit—Oklahoma, Kansas, and Texas—were called the Dust Bowl.

A NEW DEAL

In 1932, President Franklin D. Roosevelt pledged "a new deal for the American people." He pushed legislation through Congress to provide a minimum wage, unemployment insurance, and an old-age pension called Social Security. New Deal programs also put people back to work, constructing roads and buildings, clearing slums, and planting trees.

WAR AND PEACE

As the liberator of allied nations in both World War I and II, the United States has become a superpower, a model for democratic government, and a peace-keeping nation.

A DISTANT EVENT

With Europe an ocean away, World War I was "a distant event" in the mind of many Americans. Hoping to continue trade with both Britain and Germany, President Woodrow Wilson issued a proclamation of neutrality in the war. But as more and more American lives were lost at sea to German submarine attacks, neutrality was difficult to maintain. Wilson finally broke diplomatic relations with Germany. Then, in March 1917, several American ships were sunk and the nation learned of a German plot to convince Mexico to invade the U.S. Americans were outraged. On April 2, Wilson asked Congress for a declaration of war.

A COSTLY VICTORY

The U.S. entered World War II in 1941, when the Japanese bombed Pearl Harbor in the Hawaiian Islands. In the fight against Hitler's Nazi Germany and an imperialist Japan, the U.S. lost more than 300,000 soldiers. In August 1945, after Germany had surrendered on May 7, President Harry Truman ordered the dropping of atom bombs on the Japanese cities of Hiroshima and Nagasaki. Japan surrendered soon after.

▲ UNITED NATIONS

On October 24, 1945, the United Nations' charter went into effect. The new organization would enforce world peace through diplomatic, economic, and military action. UN headquarters are located in New York City.

THE COLD WAR

The Soviet Union and the United States emerged from World War II as dominant superpowers. Although never engaging each other militarily, the two nations began competing for influence in the rest of the world, particularly in developing countries. Known as the Cold War, this competition spurred a nuclear arms race that lasted 40 years and made atomic holocaust seem inevitable. A crisis occurred in October 1962, when Soviet missiles were spied on the island of Cuba. The Soviets eventually withdrew the missiles, and the U.S. promised not to invade Cuba.

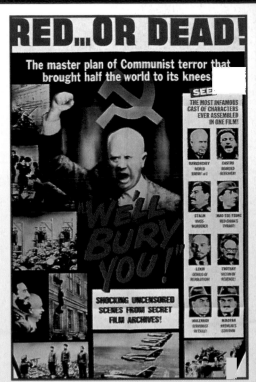

This propaganda poster highlights how distrustful the U.S. was of the communist government in the Soviet Union during the Cold War.

AT WAR WITH COMMUNISM

The U.S. fought in Korea (1950-53) and in Vietnam (1965-75) (*above*) to combat the spread of communism.

THE RED SCARE

In 1950, Senator Joseph McCarthy claimed that 205 communists were working in the U.S. State Department. McCarthy never proved a single case, but his Red Scare created an atmosphere of hysteria that wrecked many people's reputations. His fellow senators finally censured him for misconduct.

THE SPACE RACE

One positive result of U.S.-Soviet competition was space exploration. In 1961, after Soviet cosmonaut Yuri Gagarin became the first person to travel in space, President John F. Kennedy challenged Americans to land a man on the moon. A project involving 400,000 people at a cost of $22 billion, the *Apollo* 11 mission put Neil Armstrong onto the lunar dust on July 20, 1969.

A TIME FOR CHANGE

Racial segregation continued even in northern states after the Civil War, despite three constitutional amendments meant to protect the rights of newly freed slaves. In 1909, black leadership formed the National Association for the Advancement of Colored People (NAACP) to push for civil rights.

BUS BOYCOTT ▲

On December 1, 1955, Rosa Parks was arrested in Montgomery, Alabama, for refusing to give up her seat on the bus to a white man. Dr. Martin Luther King, Jr., led a successful boycott of the city's buses. In a landmark decision that helped dismantle racial segregation, the Supreme Court ruled in 1956 that segregation on buses was unconstitutional.

"I HAVE A DREAM"

At the Lincoln Memorial in 1963, before a crowd of 250,000 people, Dr. Martin Luther King, Jr., challenged the nation with a stirring speech: "I have a dream" he said, "that my four little children will one day live in a nation where they will not be judged by the color of their skin but by the content of their character." In 1964, King received the Nobel Peace Prize for his nonviolent crusade for social justice and racial harmony. He was killed by an assassin's bullet on April 4, 1968.

EQUAL SCHOOLS ▲

In the South, blacks and whites had to attend separate schools. Then, on May 17, 1954, the Supreme Court ruled that separate facilities for blacks and whites were unequal and, therefore, unconstitutional. Even so, many states resisted change. In 1957, President Eisenhower had to send in National Guard troops to protect black students entering a white school in Little Rock, Arkansas.

THE PEACE MOVEMENT

Students helped organize the first antiwar "teach-in," held at the University of Michigan in 1965, just one week after the first U.S. troops landed in South Vietnam. Protests increased as casualty lists grew longer. When President Richard Nixon ordered the invasion of Cambodia in November 1970, 300,000 war protesters marched on Washington—it was the largest demonstration in the nation's history.

GREAT SOCIETY

President Lyndon B. Johnson's crusade to create a "Great Society" was the most extensive program of social reform since Roosevelt's New Deal. It produced Medicare, Medicaid, and the first major federal-aid package for education in the U.S. But the Vietnam War—which cost over $2 billion per month by 1966—diminished Johnson's achievement.

With Jacqueline Kennedy by his side, Lyndon B. Johnson was sworn into office aboard *Air Force One* on November 22, 1963, the day President John F. Kennedy was assassinated.

EQUAL RIGHTS

In 1923, the Woman's Party proposed to Congress an equal rights amendment that would prohibit discrimination on the basis of one's sex. An equal rights amendment (ERA) was passed by both houses of Congress in March 1972, but failed when three states refused to ratify it. ERA supporters claim that women in 1990 were still earning only two thirds of what men earned for the same job.

27

GOING GLOBAL

Despite tragic setbacks and political scandals, the last decades of the 20th century saw America become the most powerful of all nations. The United States has led the world in technology and finance, provided aid to disaster-stricken countries, and advanced the cause of human rights.

▼ WATERGATE

Certain to be removed from office for his involvement in the Watergate scandal, President Richard M. Nixon, on August 8, 1974, became the first U.S. president to resign. The House of Representatives had recommended three articles of impeachment against Nixon— conspiracy to obstruct justice, abuse of power, and defiance of committee subpoenas.

LIVE AID

In 1985, a crowd of 90,000 assembled in Philadelphia's JFK Stadium, and another 1.5 billion watched the live television broadcast of the pop-music concert known as Live-Aid. More than $70 million was raised for famine relief in drought-stricken Africa.

CYBERPHILIA

Only 4,000 computers existed worldwide in 1961—all of them large, slow machines. Small silicon chips carrying electronic circuits made the computer revolution possible. The first personal computer, the Altair 8800, appeared in 1975.

▲ NUCLEAR TREATY

In December 1987, President Ronald Reagan and Soviet President Mikhail Gorbachev signed the Intermediate Nuclear Forces Treaty, promising to remove all medium and short-range missiles in Europe. It was a strong sign that the Cold War arms race was coming to an end.

▼ TRAGIC END

NASA's space-shuttle program, begun in the 1970s, designed a reusable space vehicle that could return to Earth and land like an airplane. On January 28, 1986, tragedy struck as the *Challenger* shuttle exploded just 73 seconds after lift-off, killing all seven crewmembers.

SAVING THE LAND

The United States suffered its worst oil spill ever when the tanker *Exxon-Valdez* ran aground in Alaska's Prince William Sound in March 1989. The spill of 240,000 barrels of crude oil killed so much wildlife in the region, the federal government passed new laws to protect the environment.

◄ CLINTON IMPEACHED!

On December 19, 1998, the House of Representatives impeached President Bill Clinton on charges of lying under oath to a federal grand jury and obstructing justice while under investigation by an independent counsel. Clinton is only the second president in U.S. history to be impeached. He was acquitted by the Senate on February 12, 1999.